REDISCOVERING GRACE

REDISCOVERING GRACE

SERAPHINA BLAKE

CONTENTS

Chapter 1: Introduction

Embracing Grace and Love

The Bible speaks of grace as God's unearned and undeserved favor upon believers, revealing His infinite and unfailing love for His children. This book aims to delve deeper into the concept of God's grace, portraying it not merely as unmerited favor, but as active love—love that is profound beyond human understanding. It is a love demonstrated through the sacrifice of His only Son, a love that continuously reaches out to His children despite their attitudes and behavior. This love is patient, protective, trusting, hopeful, persevering, and unfailing (1 Corinthians 13:7-8). God desires for us to walk in this love and to extend it to others. Sadly, many Christians struggle to experience God's unconditional love due to feelings of guilt and condemnation. However, true love for God begins with knowing and receiving His love: "We love because he first loved us" (1 John 4:19).

Understanding Grace

A proper understanding of grace is crucial for embracing God's love. Misunderstood, grace can be misused as a license to sin with the expectation of forgiveness. The Bible warns against this misuse: "What shall we say, then? Shall we go on sinning so that grace may increase? By no means! We died to sin; how can we live in it any longer?" (Romans 6:1-2). Additionally, grace can evoke feelings of guilt because it is unmerited. More than forgiveness and mercy, grace reflects a God who has set His heart on His rebellious and stubborn people. It is not a compartmentalized divine activity but an intrinsic part of God's character.

Throughout Christian history, grace has been defined and understood in various ways. Commonly, it is known as "God's unmerited favor," highlighting that it is free and cannot be earned or forfeited. Many people, including Christians, misunderstand grace, perceiving it as "too good to be true." It is always needed and wanted but never deserved. The hymn writer Edward Mote expressed that grace is sought on this earth, and only in Heaven will we fully realize its extent.

The Importance of Embracing God's Love

The essence of Christianity is the love of God. Despite this knowledge, many struggle to grasp its significance and to find the peace and joy that come from embracing it. While we can discuss, study, and teach about God's love, truly accepting it into our lives is often a different challenge. God's love is beyond human comprehension, but knowing it in our hearts is crucial for our relationship with Him. Embracing His love brings the peace and joy every Christian seeks, serving as the foundation for personal growth and motivating a life of obedience. It is the light at the end of the tunnel and the encouragement that sustains us through trials and despair. Embracing God's love also protects us from returning to legalism, leading us into a closer and more intimate relationship with our Heavenly Father.

Chapter 2: The Power of Grace

Overcoming Shame and Guilt

At some point in our lives, we all feel the weight of shame for something we've done, leading to a guilty conscience—a burden many carry daily. This guilt often hampers our relationships with God and others. Yet, through the blood of Jesus Christ, we are justified and reconciled to God. Justification, a gift of grace, means we are acquitted of our guilt and can find peace with God. This grace is undeserved and cannot be earned; it is only through Jesus that we can receive it. The relief of having our guilty burden removed is profound. Holding onto guilt when God has forgiven us reflects a lack of faith in God's power to save. To overcome guilt, we must believe in our justification by God's grace, as there is no condemnation for those in Christ Jesus.

Overcoming Guilt and Shame Through Grace

Grace is a transformative power that can change our lives. We were once spiritually dead in our disobedience and sins. However, God's rich mercy and great love have made us alive in Christ, saving us by grace and raising us up to sit in heavenly places with Him. This understanding leads to real repentance. Many people turn to God in "repentance" but continue to act as if they are spiritually dead. True repentance, understanding God's grace, restores complete joy. David, in deep despair after committing terrible sins, repented and asked for God's forgiveness. Filled with joy, he said, "Restore to me the joy of your salvation, and uphold me with your generous Spirit."

Experiencing the Transformative Power of Grace

The concept of "work before we receive" has often clouded our understanding of grace. Philip Yancey uses the parable of the prodigal son to illustrate God's grace. The younger son squandered his inheritance but was met with a feast upon his return. Yancey describes this as illogical love—the father forgave his son fully the moment he left home. Rembrandt's painting, "The Return of the Prodigal Son," shows the son's shame met by his father's tender countenance. Henri Nouwen's book explores his spiritual journey towards accepting God's love without earning it. Nouwen's daily prayers before the painting helped him embrace God's grace as an already existing love. Yancey, Nouwen, and others highlight the importance of accepting God's love and grace, which cannot be earned but is freely given. God loves and accepts us regardless of our past or future actions.

Finding Freedom in God's Unconditional Love

Understanding God's grace is essential to overcoming guilt and shame. When we repent with truly sorrowful hearts, grace assures the removal of our guilt. Despite deserving punishment, we are justified freely by God's grace through Jesus Christ, who was a sacrifice of atonement. Our conscience, a gift from God, convicts us of sin. When plagued by guilt, it leads to remorse, self-condemnation, and shame, damaging our self-image. Some may try to justify wrongdoing or bury feelings of guilt, while others carry deep-rooted shame from abuse and mistreatment.

Embracing the New Covenant of Grace

A proper understanding of grace is necessary to avoid being enslaved to law and legalism. Many Christians attend churches that emphasize legalism rather than the character and meaning of God's grace. They often live frustrating lives of defeat and failure, instead of the abundant life Jesus promised. My own experience with criticism over running a marathon taught me this lesson. After writing about the event for a Christian magazine, I received numerous letters criticizing my involvement, claiming it was "a waste of time" or "unworthy of a Christian." This incident highlighted the importance of understanding and embracing God's grace rather than adhering to legalistic views.

Chapter 3: Rediscovering God's Love

Reflecting on the Nature of God's Love

Most Christians are aware that God loves them, but how deeply has this truth really permeated our hearts? There is a significant difference between mental assent and heart revelation. Many are blinded to the profound knowledge of Christ's love because they haven't grasped the true nature of God's love. Viewing God as harsh, austere, or quick to punish causes our hearts to pull away from Him. However, 1 John 4:8,16 explains, "God is Love. He who does not love does not know God, for God is love... and we have known and believed the love that God has for us." The challenge lies in truly believing this truth. Often, we measure God's love by our blessings or trials and forget that Christ's work justifies God's great love for us, proving once and for all that nothing in us can repel His love. This chapter will explore the facets of God's love, using many scriptural references to reveal the amazing truth that God loves us.

The following chapters will guide readers on an insightful journey into the very heart of God; to rediscover the knowledge of His nature of love and revel in the immeasurable depth of His love for us as His people. It is through our personal revelation of the glorified

Christ that our hearts can be truly won over, and God's sovereignty in our lives firmly established. As Watchman Nee says, "The more you realize the nature of God, the more you realize there is nothing in yourself whereby you can please Him." This lack of understanding of the true nature of God is the underlying issue for every Christian.

Reflecting in Theological Contexts

Reflection in theological contexts involves seeking deeper meaning in phenomena, particularly God's word. The assumption is that God's communication to humanity has been recorded in sacred texts (logos). Through reflection, the presence of God is revealed in understanding what has been communicated. Though reflection usually occurs within the Christian tradition, the assumption of a communicative God means it shouldn't be limited to scripture. God's presence can be reflected upon in the created world, allowing natural theology to have a place in theological reflection.

Reflection is also an ongoing process of thought and action, not merely a look back at past actions. It involves critiquing assumptions and determining actions based on current understanding—a continued dialectic of understanding and action. This is crucial in practical theology, which bases actions on understanding God. Reflection assumes a separation from the phenomenon being reflected upon, challenging when reflecting on one's present existence in God's presence. Reflection and action can become concurrent, where action is undertaken to improve understanding and better guide future actions. Reflection often requires learning, leading to transformation—a goal of theological actions guided by God's will.

Reconnecting with God's Love in Everyday Life

All of life is connected to God's love, not just during crises. We must seek the divine embrace in every situation. For instance, when a child reaches out for comfort despite misbehavior, it reflects God's desire for us to return to Him despite our shortcomings. God, like a parent, longs to embrace us, offering love and peace despite our shame. His love is unchanging, pursuing us from everlasting to everlasting. This love is intricately linked to the cross of Christ, demonstrated through Jesus' sacrifice for us while we were still sinners. This great love deserves full recognition and is vital for believers at every stage of their spiritual journey.

Life's busyness often crowds out the comforting presence of God. We juggle family, work, and responsibilities, forgetting that God wants to be involved in every aspect of our lives. We must break the false division between secular and sacred, living all aspects of life in conscious awareness of the living God and a life of faith.

Embracing God's Love in Times of Struggle

For many, embracing God's love during struggles is the hardest part of their spiritual journey. Yet, it is in these dark times that we must hold onto God's love. Clinging to His promises, despite our circumstances, helps us refute the enemy's lies that God's love has abandoned us. Failure to embrace God's love during hardships can lead to a sense of abandonment, resulting in anger, bitterness, and deeper despair. It is crucial to continue believing in God's love, regardless of our emotions. Our emotions may not align with the truth, so we must actively fight to cling to the hope that His love will bring us through to better times.

Chapter 4: Embracing Grace in Relationships

The Impact of Words

Consider the last argument you had with someone. Who won? What was the outcome of that argument? Was it a success for both parties, or did someone lose? Perhaps it left a bitter taste or a deep sense of regret. Words, once spoken, cannot be taken back, and we can never truly know their impact on the other person. In any relationship between two imperfect individuals, there will be moments when grace is needed. However, showing grace is not always easy. In the heat of the moment, the natural instinct is to lash out. It takes great self-discipline and strength of character to hold back and show grace, especially when you feel wronged. But doing so can avert much heartache and anger. In the long run, showing grace instead of anger or bitterness can only strengthen a relationship and bring glory to God.

Extending Grace to Others

It's essential to distinguish between forgiveness and reconciliation. Imagine a wife who has been beaten by her husband; if she tells the pastor she's terrified and plans to leave, it's right to advise against reconciliation. The husband needs to repent and receive forgiveness, but that forgiveness doesn't mean everything returns to normal. He must face the legal consequences of his actions and prove, through a change in behavior over time, that he is safe to be around. This is an example of the wife loving her husband by taking a tough stance for his long-term benefit. She's willing to forgive and encourage him but not to pretend nothing happened.

One critical application of grace in relationships is loving others as God loves us. This means accepting others and offering the same forgiveness we've received. It requires us to intentionally set aside our needs and feelings to focus on others. By helping them make constructive changes, we can further the work of grace in their lives. The vital starting point in extending grace to others is recognizing our sinfulness and God's ongoing forgiveness toward us.

Healing Broken Relationships Through Grace

The power of forgiveness in healing relationships cannot be overstated, and grace and forgiveness go hand in hand. Without understanding God's forgiveness and grace toward us in Christ, it is impossible to offer forgiveness and grace to those who have wronged us. Grace removes the guilt and anger hindering reconciliation and makes healing possible. As we grow in understanding the great debt forgiven us, we can more freely forgive those who have sinned against us, knowing our righteousness does not justify us any more than theirs justifies them.

Broken relationships are a universal human experience, often lasting a lifetime or passing through generations. The pain of damaged relationships is all too real, revealing the effects of sin and the fall. Healing our relationships with others is one area where the refreshing power of God's grace can be most powerfully experienced.

Cultivating a Grace-Filled Community

Creating a grace-filled community is the natural culmination of extending grace and healing broken relationships. A community characterized by grace is a safe place where imperfection is accepted, and grace is offered and expected. Failure is not met with fatalism but with the understanding that we are all on a journey. It's a safe place to admit our shortcomings and temptations, to confess our sins. Confidentiality is guarded, and sins are met with prayer and support, not condemnation. It's a safe place to change, allowing the space for transformation.

Most importantly, a grace-filled community is a safe place to be vulnerable. In many Christian circles, vulnerability is risky. Revealing your true self can be unsafe, especially if you've been hurt in the past. Yet, the body of Christ should be precisely where this happens. If grace is truly understood and embraced, it will result in a community quick to offer love and acceptance, no matter what is uncovered.

Chapter 5: Living a Grace-Filled Life

Understanding Grace as a Free Gift

After completing university, many face the pressure to "make something of themselves" in their professional careers. This worldly mentality of earning one's way into a good life is countered by the concept of grace as a free gift. Donald Miller's exhortation to "bind our shattered lives together with one unity, that in the ages to come He might show the surpassing riches of His grace" serves as a reminder that our lives are not something to be earned. Step one to living a grace-filled life is surrendering to the reality that we cannot earn grace; accepting this helps us receive the best that God has to offer.

In his section "Surrendering to God's Grace," Miller explains how the world tempts people to believe they can buy grace through conduct or living. He emphasizes that grace "can be bought only with the precious blood of Christ." To imagine we can earn it shows a misunderstanding of grace, which is the free, undeserved goodness of God. The first step in accepting God's grace is recognizing that it can only be received as a gift. Failing to understand this means missing out on the best in life, simply because we have not grasped the goodness of God.

Surrendering to God's Grace

Personal grudges hinder life and relationships. Comparing the Christian walk to the depth of forgiveness received in Christ highlights the importance of forgiveness. Christ died so the world could be forgiven; Christians only forgive when they grasp their own forgiven sins and taste the resulting freedom. Practical steps include defining forgiveness, addressing repeat offenders, and realizing that not forgiving hinders their own forgiveness. Christians should expect God to forgive them as they forgive others. Empathy with God's standard of forgiveness helps move through the painful process of forgiving. Letting go of bitterness is vital, as it can veil one's view of the world. Practical suggestions for dealing with past hurts are compared to cleaning wounds so they heal correctly.

Embracing Forgiveness and Letting Go of Bitterness

Forgiving others brings freedom and allows God to work in wondrous ways, replacing festering bitterness with joy (2 Corinthians 2:10-11). God provides a way to forgive those who have wronged us. Understanding God's forgiveness towards us motivates us to forgive others. The parable of the unforgiving servant (Matthew 18:23-35) illustrates this. Forgiveness is a command for believers, and failure to forgive can lead to God's discipline and hindered prayer life.

Bitterness consumes and destroys, rendering one ineffective in service to God. It causes people to focus on past pain, failing to solve the hurt. Many feed upon their bitterness, repeating the offense in their minds until it takes hold of their lives.

Nurturing a Heart of Gratitude and Humility

A heart touched by God's love and grace is not self-righteous or condemning. Awareness of one's sin and God's favor results in dependence on God and confidence in His mercy. This contrasts with the self-righteous person who views themselves as deserving of God's blessing and looks down on others. Growing in understanding God's grace leads to compassion and forgiveness towards others, slow to anger or judgment, aware of personal weaknesses and God's patience.

Though Christians experience God's grace at the cross, gratitude often wanes as life's realities press in. Many are driven to God by duty and guilt, not enjoyment and freedom in response to His grace. This is a tragic error, denying the gospel of grace by seeking to earn salvation and blessings rather than receiving them as free gifts from God.

Chapter 6: Embracing Grace in Adversity

The Presence of Adversity

Throughout our lives, we inevitably face adversity. Financial hardships, physical ailments, and emotional distress can all test our faith and love the most. During such times, we might question how a loving God can allow these difficulties. Yet, it's essential to remember that God's grace is sufficient for us; His power is made perfect in weakness. Though we might not always understand why adversity occurs, we can be assured that God is with us every step of the way and does not abandon us. In the face of trials, we should seek God in prayer, just as Jesus did in the Garden of Gethsemane. Overwhelmed with sorrow, Jesus found strength and trust in God's plan through prayer, which we can emulate to find assurance of God's presence and the strength to endure.

Finding Strength and Hope in Difficult Times

Believing that God is for us during adversity can be challenging. Reasoning from our experiences to God's attitude toward us is a common mistake. I've spoken to individuals who stopped going to church, believing that God was against them because of their life struggles. In adversity, it's tempting to replay feelings of abandonment by God. However, during these times, it's crucial to preach the gospel to ourselves and find God's grace amidst suffering. Understanding that God's grace is a present reality in our lives, even when life is full of losses and crosses, is vital. People who are suffering don't need explanations; they need to find God's grace in their pain.

Trusting in God's Grace During Trials

Trusting in God's grace means believing that God has a plan for us, even during hard times. Christians have faith that trials might lead to something better, even if the purpose isn't clear. Trusting in His wisdom and love means believing that He wants the best for us and that all experiences, good or bad, serve His purpose. This grace and purpose extend beyond this lifetime. Titus 2:11 reminds us that "the grace of God that brings salvation has appeared to all men." Grace is not just for making life better now but ensures our future with God, free from worldly trials.

Trials test and refine the human spirit. For Christians, it's not just a test of character but of faith in God. Immediate reactions to adversity, such as anger or despair, don't signify a lack of faith but remind us of our weakness and dependence on God. 2 Corinthians tells us, "My grace is sufficient for you, for my power is made perfect in weakness." Trusting in God's grace during adversity is a conscious effort to depend on Him, believing that His love and grace are active forces in our lives.

Growing in Faith Through Adversity

Rick's gratitude for prayers during his difficult times, hoping for increased grace and wisdom, exemplifies an uncommon but vital attitude. Often, people question God during trials, asking why it's happening to them. Rick views trials as tests of faith, revealing weaknesses that need improvement. These trials refine our faith, deepen dependence on Christ, and develop Christ-like character. James 3:17 states, "But the wisdom that comes from heaven is first of all pure;

then peace-loving, considerate, submissive, full of mercy and good fruit, impartial and sincere." Adversity tests and grows our faith, leading us to deeper reliance on God.

Chapter 7: Grace in Action

The Call to Action

The only valid response to learning about God's unconditional love and grace is to put it into action. The world desperately needs a practical demonstration of this kind of love, and it will only see it when God's people intentionally and strategically live it out wherever they are. This is putting grace into action; it shows faith in God's character and Christ's work, proving that life with Him is better than anywhere else. Grace-filled actions—service and love in tangible forms—bring glory to God, declaring His goodness and love. Anyone can do good works, but the goal is to be a doer of God's work. This occurs as believers allow Christ to live through them by the power of the Holy Spirit. This is vital for impacting the world for God. Doing our own thing in His name is easy, but the only activity bearing fruit for eternity is that which Jesus initiates and completes.

Practicing Acts of Grace and Kindness

Practicing grace is foundational, yet it's unnatural for us. We often focus on payback and getting what we deserve. Grace is a free gift, and accepting it means admitting our sin. Realizing we are sinners saved by grace should humble us and eliminate spiritual pride. Because I've been saved by grace, I can no longer look down on others. Practicing acts of grace and kindness involves extending favor to someone, whether they deserve it or not. This can be achieved in practical ways, primarily through words. Build others up rather than criticize and tear down. Encourage rather than nag. Speak kind words rather than harsh ones. Can you accept a reproof, given graciously, with humility? True grace also goes easy on the faults of others.

Sharing God's Love Through Service

How do we share God's love through service? By actively seeking opportunities to love and serve others with a gracious spirit. The first step is cultivating an attitude of service. Develop eyes to see others' needs and ears to hear their cries for help. These needs are all around us—in our homes, workplaces, churches, neighborhoods, and communities. The second step is making a conscious effort to meet others' needs, often by giving of our time. Set aside a few hours a week to volunteer for a cause. Some may be called to give up certain lifestyles or careers to serve others. Spending time with God in prayer and seeking counsel helps us discern what specific act of service God may ask of us. Throughout it all, remain humble and rely on God, recognizing that His grace enables us to serve. Verse 9 of our key passage teaches us that "we are God's workmanship, created in Christ Jesus to do good works, which God prepared in advance for us to do." The Greek word for workmanship is 'poiema,' from which we get 'poem,' meaning a masterpiece. This verse teaches that as God's creation in Christ Jesus, our lives should be works of art, reflecting His love and grace through our actions.

Impacting the World Through Grace-Filled Actions

Lives have been transformed, and households reconciled due to the ministry of Christians involved with GYMN. One impactful story is a couple from Russia whose 10-year-old daughter was murdered. The GYMN intern in Russia ministered to this couple, helping them connect with God through their married life, diving into His word and prayer. The Holy Spirit blessed the couple with the assurance of salvation and the hope of seeing their daughter again in heaven.

Christ offers hope to abandon criticalness and act as Jesus would. Many students have taken the Christian Youth in Action training and found their lives changed. We are molding tomorrow's leaders through the heritage of support GYMN provides these youth.

Chapter 8: Embracing Grace in Self-Acceptance

The Journey to Self-Acceptance

Self-acceptance requires replacing old tapes of self-rejection with new ones of who we are in Christ. Our identity in Him is a settled issue, and God has secured our worth with His love. Therefore, we can label our sins as what we do, not who we are. Christ has struck at the root of our feelings of unworthiness by making us worthy with His worthiness. Through His redemption, He makes us acceptable to God because He accepts us. This grace, this unmerited favor, assures us that nothing we do can make God love us more or less. We have God's total approval.

We recognize our imperfections but keep a list of our flaws, unconsciously thinking less of ourselves when we don't measure up. Perfectionists struggle with addiction and depression because who they are never matches who they want to be. This rejection of self fails to grasp our acceptance by a God who loves us in our weakness.

The pervasive human condition is that we don't believe we're worthy of love and acceptance. The world's answer to feelings of inadequacy is to try harder. The greater our unworthiness, the harder we try to feel acceptable, leading to perfectionism. At the root of perfectionism is the idea that earning acceptance and approval makes us acceptable to others and ourselves.

Do you love yourself? Most would say yes, but many struggle with self-rejection. I recall a time when I truly disliked myself, which led to a breakdown. Realizing this was far more than not loving oneself—it was total self-rejection.

Letting Go of Perfectionism and Embracing Grace

Perfectionism separates us from God, convincing us He isn't a God for imperfect people like us. If we fail academically, we feel we've failed God and have no worth. We must remind ourselves that God loves us even more when we fail. He knows our failures and weaknesses, yet still loves us.

Instead of trying to be perfect, run the race with endurance—an undertaking never achieved. Striving for perfection goes against belief in Christ, who is perfect for us. We live in a flawed world, and striving for perfection binds us to burdens rather than the easy yoke of Jesus. Perfect performance becomes our primary measurement of self-worth, a value borrowed from the world. Christ gives us intrinsic worth not based on accomplishments, true on our worst day. Performance-based self-worth causes some to question their worthiness as Christians, separating them from God.

Embracing Self-Compassion and Love

Self-judgment and self-condemnation destroy our peace. Fallen humanity is vulnerable to self-hatred, often displeased with ourselves for being sinners. This is projected onto God and others, feeling we're in God's bad books. If we run from God, we find the judge still in pursuit.

But our Lord's words are clear: "Do not judge and you will not be judged. Do not condemn and you will not be condemned. Forgive and you will be forgiven." Often, what we judge and condemn in others is what we condemn in ourselves. Our self-condemnation cries out for forgiveness and assurance of non-condemnation.

Judgment is unavoidable; we all do it in society and churches. Some establish what constitutes good behavior and ensure it's lived up to, often resulting in criticism felt even if unspoken.

Recognizing Our Worthiness in God's Eyes

We can't argue that we're worthy of a love that sent Christ to die for us while we were sinners and enemies of God. We were children of wrath, conducted in our lusts, and had become worthless. All have sinned and fall short of God's glory. In light of these truths, we're not worthy of such love, yet it's in seeing these truths that we fully appreciate God's grace.

It's not about recognizing our worthiness. It's not about our behavior or accomplishments. It's about unearned, undeserved, unmerited favor. It's about who God is and His nature. Our behavior, sins, good deeds, faith, or obedient heart don't affect God's love for us.

Chapter 9: Conclusion

Embracing God's Unconditional Love and Grace

Millions across the globe live in fear that God is still angry at them. Grace often remains hidden due to its foreignness to the natural man and is often lost under religious tradition and expectation. There is much to teach and preach about God's grace. The love of God was unleashed through Jesus Christ in a staggering display of love and kindness. We must stand in this truth and teach it. Many people, perhaps even you, are hurting under the misconception that God is angry at them. But consider this: if the worst sinner received grace as a free gift, we no longer need to earn it. Grace is indeed too good to be true—that's what makes it grace. It thrills us to realize that we are loved despite not deserving it. This grace can melt away guilt and shame, even putting addictions to death. But to believe it, we must first understand it. Embrace a deep understanding of God's love and grace; meditate on and pray for this understanding. It could be revolutionary for you.

Everything wonderful we receive in Jesus Christ is accessible through knowing Him. To understand God's love and grace in Jesus is to be complete in Christ. It's crucial to differentiate between Law and Grace, love and condemnation, Jesus Christ and religion. By understanding this, we can point ourselves and others back to God.

Let us boldly approach the throne of grace, encouraging and helping one another, especially when confronting God's true character. Doing so will bring colossal change, a reformation within the Church. This change will enable a lost and dying world to see the throbbing heart of God through Jesus Christ. Thus, it is vital for the Church to reach out to the lost and lonely, sharing an understanding of true love and mercy.

Embracing a Grace-Centered Life

Live under grace, not law. Learn to ignore the advice of friends, relatives, and even fellow Christians when it is law-oriented. Refuse to be pressured by others or your accusative conscience. Accept yourself as you are; you are acceptable to God. Don't accept the idea that you are being punished through adverse circumstances because of a particular sin. Remember the cross of Christ—the penalty has been paid. "There is now no condemnation for those who are in Christ Jesus." Step out from under the cloud of guilt, resentment, and hostility.

Realize that you are a new person. Regardless of your life situation or past actions, remind yourself that you are a new person in Christ. The old has gone, the new has come. Entertain no notions to the contrary. Integrate a grace perspective into your life with these suggestions:

1. Refuse to accept law-oriented advice or accusations.
2. Remember and internalize that you are a new person in Christ.
3. Step out from guilt and resentment; accept yourself as God does.

Encouragement to Share God's Love and Grace with Others

As we conclude, let's explore how to share God's great love with others. Sharing God's love can be done in countless ways, big and small. Seek to be an instrument of God's peace and grace in the world, communicating love through word and action. Since love is the heart of the message of grace, it is important for Christians to understand what it means to love. Love as Christ loved us, with a sacrificial love. "Be imitators of God, therefore, as dearly loved children and live a life of love, just as Christ loved us and gave himself up for us as a fragrant offering and sacrifice to God" (Ephesians 5:1-2).

Loving as Christ did means loving the unlovable and those who don't "deserve" to be loved. This challenging calling clearly communicates that nothing can separate a person from God's love. When God's love is shown to those "far away," it calls them back to the Lord. Love must be accompanied by forgiveness. Many are turned away from Christianity by judgmental and unforgiving Christians. Failing to understand grace makes it difficult to forgive others, leading to quick condemnation of fellow Christians who sin. This reflects an attitude God has never held toward His children. When we sin, God doesn't turn away in anger and disgust. Instead, He waits for our return and meets us with open arms and great joy. The parable of the prodigal son illustrates this beautifully. When the son returns, the father is filled with compassion, runs to meet him, and welcomes him back as a son. This is how God always receives us.